PIONEERS OF EQUALITY

BY JIM OLLHOFF

VISIT US AT
WWW.ABDOPUBLISHING.COM

Published by ABDO Publishing Company, 8000 West 78th Street, Suite 310, Edina, MN 55439. Copyright ©2011 by Abdo Consulting Group, Inc. International copyrights reserved in all countries. No part of this book may be reproduced in any form without written permission from the publisher. ABDO & Daughters™ is a trademark and logo of ABDO Publishing Company.

Printed in the United States of America, North Mankato, Minnesota.
112010
012011

 PRINTED ON RECYCLED PAPER

Editor: John Hamilton
Graphic Design: John Hamilton
Cover Design: Neil Klinepier
Cover Photo: Getty Images
Interior Photos and Illustrations: Corbis-pgs 6-7, 9; Getty Images-pgs 10, 16, 17, 18, 23; Granger Collection-pgs 4-5, 8, 11, 14, 15, 19, 20, 21, 22, 25, 26-27, 28-29; iStock-photo-pgs 12-13; ThinkStock-pg 24.

Library of Congress Cataloging-in-Publication Data

Ollhoff, Jim, 1959-
  Pioneers of equality / Jim Ollhoff.
    p. cm. -- (African-American history)
  Includes index.
  ISBN 978-1-61714-712-8
  1. African Americans--Biography--Juvenile literature. 2. African Americans--History--1877-1964--Juvenile literature. I. Title.
  E185.6.O55 2011
  920.009296073--dc22

                        2010038369

CONTENTS

AFTER THE CIVIL WAR

The horrors of slavery in the United States ended after the Civil War. However, African Americans still had a long way to go on the road to equality. Racism is a disease that dies slowly, and the years after the Civil War were difficult for the newly freed slaves.

Many blacks were suddenly free, but they had no money. They still had to work for Southern farmers. Many blacks worked on plantations and received part of the profits from the crops. This was called sharecropping. If the crops were good, the sharecroppers got more money. If the crops were poor, the sharecroppers received less money. Under this scheme, everyone was motivated to take care of the crops. The problem was that the farmers were sometimes dishonest with their bookkeeping. They short-changed the black workers by not giving them their fair share.

Many African Americans moved north, out of the old Confederate states. However, people who owned Northern businesses felt threatened by the large population of black workers. People were afraid the black workers would take their jobs. In many places, African Americans were forced to take menial, low-paying jobs.

A 13-year-old sharecropper near Americus, Georgia. An oil painting over a photograph by Dorothea Lange, taken in 1937.

In many places, successful black business owners were run out of town by angry whites, simply because the black businesses were hurting the businesses of the white owners. Sometimes, blacks were beaten or killed by angry mobs. The Ku Klux Klan, composed of racist whites, terrorized black Americans, often preventing them from voting or other activities.

Blacks who were convicted of small crimes were often given unusually long prison sentences. They could be chained together and loaned to companies that used them for free labor. These "chain gangs" often spent all day working in the hot sun for no money.

Life continued to be segregated, or separated. Blacks were not allowed to ride certain buses, go to certain schools, or shop at certain businesses. In some places, there would be a public drinking fountain for white people and a separate drinking fountain for black people. Segregation was the common practice for almost 100 years after the Civil War.

Despite the racism, inequality, and prejudice, voices for change arose. Some African Americans were gifted in the arts or sports. Some were brilliant in medicine and science. Some were creative inventors. Some blacks led others with their intellect and moral bravery. Others were gifted teachers. It became increasingly difficult for racists to say that blacks were inferior. All people, no matter what skin color, owe a debt of gratitude to the pioneers in the following pages.

A segregated water fountain in the American South, sometime in the 1950s.

EDUCATORS: LEADING THE WAY

After the Civil War, black Americans lived in a society where many people had racist attitudes. Further, the institutions in society kept blacks from succeeding—a process called institutional racism. African Americans often couldn't get justice in the courts. They often were forced to attend underfunded schools. They frequently received less pay in their jobs, even when they did the same work as whites.

African Americans needed strong leaders with great minds. These were people who could understand the issues and clearly say what the problems were and how to fix them. Two of the many strong leaders and educators of the time were Booker T. Washington and William E.B. Du Bois.

Booker T. Washington (1856–1915) was born in the slave state of Virginia a few years before the Civil War started. When the war ended in 1865, he and his family gained their freedom. He taught himself to read and write, and went to college. He graduated at the top of his class.

Booker T. Washington at the Tuskegee Institute in 1906.

In 1881, Alabama decided to create a school to train black teachers. It was called the Tuskegee Institute, located in Tuskegee, Alabama. Booker T. Washington was asked to run the school. He and the students built the school, both its physical structure and its curriculum. He talked about how all people needed to work to improve their own place in life. He also befriended wealthy people who helped finance the school. His friendship with wealthy former slave owners caused some people to distrust him. However, he was always interested in building bridges between people instead of walls.

Booker T. Washington reading at his desk.

William Edward Burghardt Du Bois (1868–1963) was born in Massachusetts a few years after the Civil War ended. He was a man of great intellect, becoming the first African American to earn a doctorate from Harvard University. He taught at several colleges.

Du Bois helped start a group called the Niagara Movement. Its mission was to end racial separation and discrimination. Du Bois wanted equality between people of all skin colors.

In 1909, William Du Bois helped found the National Association for the Advancement of Colored People (NAACP). The NAACP continues working today to end hate and racism.

William E.B. Du Bois, educator, editor, and writer. Oil on canvas painting by Laura Wheeler Waring.

ACTIVISTS: SPEAKING OUT AGAINST VIOLENCE

One of the most terrible ways to attack black people after the Civil War was by lynching. Lynching was an assault by out-of-control mobs that captured people and executed them without involving any police, judges, or other authorities. Usually, the person would be dragged from their home or work, and then hanged by the mob. Few people were ever arrested for being part of a lynch mob.

There were many triggers for lynching. Sometimes, a black person would be convicted of a crime, and so members of an angry mob would take punishment into their own hands. More often, the African American was only accused of a crime. Sometimes, it was not even a crime—it may have only been a desire to eat at a "whites only" restaurant.

In many places, the racist Ku Klux Klan organization used the threat of lynching as a way to keep black people from voting at the polls.

13

Ida Wells-Barnett

14

A hooded African American man with a noose around his neck is executed by a lynch mob in Carrollton, Missouri, in 1896.

One of the foremost anti-lynching crusaders was Ida Wells-Barnett (1862–1931). She was born to slaves, but grew up with a desire to create equality. She sued a railroad company after she was forcibly dragged out of her seat on the train so the seat could be given to a white person. She became a journalist in Memphis, Tennessee. In 1891, a black-owned grocery store was taking a lot of business from a nearby white-owned grocery, so a lynch mob attacked the store. Three African Americans who were friends of Ida were killed. She began an investigation of lynchings and race riots around the country. Her research convinced many whites that the lynchings were never about justice. She helped turn the tide against this kind of mob violence. Eventually, anti-lynching laws began to be passed.

Ida Wells-Barnett was a fierce and tireless crusader for equality. She said she had a dream of a society where all people "pay tribute to...qualities of mind and heart, rather than to the color of the skin."

SOLDIERS: HEROES OF THE WORLD WARS

About 370,000 African Americans became soldiers in World War I (1914–1918), but they usually fought in segregated units. Black units fought bravely alongside French soldiers. They spent time in French cities, which were largely free of the racist segregation present in much of the United States. This made coming back to the United States difficult.

During World War II (1939–1945), African Americans continued to fight in segregated units. Military bases were usually segregated, too. This meant that black soldiers couldn't use the base restaurants, theaters, or gyms. This led to many conflicts and fights on the bases.

African American soldiers fought the enemy, but they also fought racism. On both fronts, they persevered bravely.

The Tuskegee Airmen were an especially successful group of black fighters during World War II. They were pilots who trained at the Tuskegee Army Airfield, near Tuskegee, Alabama. They won many air battles in the skies over Europe. As a group, they earned 150 Distinguished Flying Crosses and three Presidential Unit Citations.

Major George Spencer Roberts, in training for the U.S. Army Air Corps 99th Pursuit Squadron, better known as the Tuskegee Airmen of World War II.

ACTORS POETS AND MUSICIANS

After World War I ended in 1918, one of the largest urban black communities was in the Harlem district of New York City. It was a mix of many groups, including Jamaicans, Haitians, Africans, and black Americans. This rich mix of cultures resulted in an explosion of creativity in literature, music, and theater. It is often referred to as the Harlem Renaissance.

Actor Paul Robeson, left, in a scene from William Shakespeare's Othello. Robeson was an acclaimed international star in theater and film. He first became famous in the 1920s during the Harlem Renaissance.

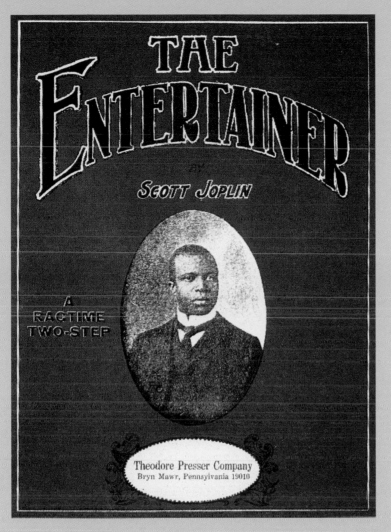

Musician Scott Joplin (c.1867–1917) was born in Texas, and spent time in Chicago, Illinois, and St. Louis, Missouri, before moving to New York City. He was one of the best piano players of his time, and became known for a type of music called ragtime. Ragtime combined old slave melodies with a fast new sound that became extremely popular for dancing as well as playing. Joplin's music helped set the stage for other black musicians, who would refine and popularize the Harlem Renaissance "sound."

In 1976, 59 years after his death, Joplin was awarded the Pulitzer Prize for his contribution to American music.

The famous poet Langston Hughes (1902–1967) emerged during the Harlem Renaissance. He wrote "The Weary Blues" in 1926. It was an attempt to write the rhythms of black speech in a style called "jazz poetry." Hughes was also a popular playwright and novelist.

Droning a drowsy syncopated tune,
Rocking back and forth to a mellow croon,
  I heard a Negro play.
Down on Lenox Avenue the other night
By the pale dull pallor of an old gas light
  He did a lazy sway . . .
  He did a lazy sway . . .
To the tune o' those Weary Blues.
—Excerpt from "The Weary Blues"

Duke Ellington, *musician and composer.*

Duke Ellington (1899–1974) was born in Washington, DC, where he formed his first band. He played ragtime, gospel, swing, and blues, but was most famous for his jazz music. He played piano and composed music. For his extraordinary life achievements, he was awarded a Pulitzer Prize, a Presidential Medal of Freedom, several Grammy Awards, and countless other awards.

Not only did the Harlem Renaissance give the world tremendous new artists and art forms, it also forced white America to look at black America differently. No longer were black Americans uneducated former slaves from the South. Now, black Americans were educated, talented, classy, and cultured. The Harlem Renaissance tore down another brick in the wall of racism.

ATHLETES: THRILLING THE WORLD

The 1936 Summer Olympic Games were held in Berlin, Germany. The leader of Germany at that time was Adolf Hitler. He believed that Aryans, or white people from northern Europe, were the best of all races. He thought his Aryan athletes would win all of the medals in the Olympics. Jesse Owens (1913–1980) had other ideas. Owens was an African American man from a poor family in Alabama. He ran track in high school and college. In the 1936 Olympics, he won gold medals in the 100-meter race, the 200-meter race, the 400-meter relay, and the long jump.

Jesse Owens at the start of the 200-meter sprint final, at the 1936 Olympic Games in Berlin, Germany.

Jackie Robinson playing for the Brooklyn Dodgers in 1947.

Jackie Robinson (1919–1972) was the first black American to play in modern Major League Baseball. In 1947, he started with the Brooklyn Dodgers. Other teams threatened to go on strike. But play continued, and Robinson knew he had to be twice as good as anyone else in order to be accepted. In 1947, he won the Rookie of the Year Award. In 1949, he won the National League's Most Valuable Player Award. In 1955, Robinson and the Dodgers won the World Series. In 1962, Robinson was inducted into the Baseball Hall of Fame.

Jesse Owens and Jackie Robinson broke through many skin-color barriers, making it easier for those who came after them. Thanks to their success, more people began to question racial segregation in other areas of society.

SCIENTISTS AND INVENTORS

The brilliant men and women of science have eased the suffering of people in countless ways. In medicine, for example, a knife wound to the chest was often considered fatal. But in 1893, Dr. Daniel Hale Williams (1856–1931) was one of the first doctors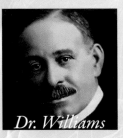

Dr. Williams

to operate on the human heart. He repaired the heart of a man who had been injured with a knife blade. Dr. Williams went on to create medical facilities for African Americans, at a time when many hospitals would not admit blacks.

Dr. Charles Drew, *African American physician and researcher.*

Another famous medical doctor was Dr. Charles Drew (1904–1950). He was born in Washington, DC, and went on through school to earn an MD and a PhD. Dr. Drew was fascinated with the problems of blood transfusions. Blood had to be used fresh, it had to be free of contamination, and the different types of blood couldn't be mixed. Dr. Drew helped find better ways to store blood. During World War II, Dr. Drew's research on blood banks and transfusions helped save the lives of many American and Allied soldiers and civilians.

One of the most famous agricultural scientists was George Washington Carver (1864–1943). Born in Missouri as a slave, he went to school in Missouri and Kansas. His college applications were rejected at first because he was black. However, he continued to apply to colleges, and finally was admitted to Simpson College in Iowa.

He eventually went to work at the Tuskegee Institute in Alabama.

Southern soils at that time were depleted of nutrients from years of growing cotton. Carver looked for ways to replenish the soil. He found that growing other crops, such as peanuts, could replenish the soil with nutrients. Then he looked for ways to use peanuts and peanut oil. He found more than 300 uses for the peanut crop. He also found ways to use sweet potatoes. He freely gave his discoveries and inventions to farmers. On his gravestone is written, "He could have added fortune and fame, but caring for neither, he found happiness and honor in being helpful to the world."

At a time when ignorance fostered the idea that blacks were inferior, people like Daniel Hale Williams, Charles Drew, and George Washington Carver helped turn the tide against racism. It became impossible to say that people with black skin were inferior when the word spread of brilliant scientists such as these.

Botanist, chemist, and educator George Washington Carver (second from right) teaching in a chemistry laboratory at the Tuskegee Institute, Alabama, in about 1906.

EXECUTIVE ORDERS

Over time, more people began to question the practice of segregation. They questioned whether it was right to treat people separately. Many people began to wonder why there was a separation between blacks and whites.

In 1941, President Franklin Roosevelt, under pressure from civil rights leaders, signed Executive Order 8802. It prohibited racial discrimination in the United States defense industry. No longer could defense companies discriminate against people because of their skin color. The executive order prohibited military job discrimination on the basis of race, creed, color, or national origin.

In 1948, President Harry Truman signed Executive Order 9981, which desegregated the military. Segregated units and bases were phased out.

These executive orders gave more fuel for those who spoke out against injustice. However, the road to equality is always long. A lot more work had to be done. Much of that work happened over the next 15 years, during a time known as the civil rights movement.

In July 1948, the Chicago Defender *hailed President Truman's signing of* Executive Order 9981.

GLOSSARY

CIVIL RIGHTS

The rights of all individuals to participate equally in their communities.

CIVIL WAR

The war fought between America's Northern and Southern states from 1861–1865. The Southern states were for slavery. They wanted to start their own country. Northern states fought against slavery and a division of the country.

CONFEDERACY

The Southern states of Alabama, Arkansas, Florida, Georgia, Louisiana, Mississippi, North Carolina, South Carolina, Tennessee, Texas, and Virginia. These states wanted to keep slavery legal. They broke away from the United States during the Civil War and formed their own country known as the Confederate States of America, or the Confederacy. The Confederacy ended in 1865 when the war ended and the 11 Confederate states rejoined the United States.

KU KLUX KLAN

Often referred to as the KKK, the Ku Klux Klan is an extreme, racist organization that believes in the supremacy of white people over all other races. It was formed in the Southern states after the Civil War. The group used violence to oppose equal rights for African Americans. KKK members often disguised themselves by dressing in white robes with hoods, and burned wooden crosses as a Klan symbol.

Lynching

When an angry mob murders someone. The lynched person was usually black, and the typical form of death was by hanging.

Plantation

A large farm where crops such as tobacco, sugar cane, and cotton are grown. It takes many people to run a plantation. Workers usually live right on the property. Early American plantation owners used cheap slave labor to make their operations more profitable.

Pulitzer Prize

An annual award for outstanding achievement in American journalism, literature, or music. Named after newspaper publisher Joseph Pulitzer.

Racism

The belief that people of one skin color are better than people of another skin color, or that individuals of a certain skin color have certain characteristics *because* of their skin color.

Renaissance

A renewed interest in something, often a revival of the arts or learning. In the Harlem Renaissance of the 1920s and 1930s, African Americans and other groups in New York City's Harlem district sparked a growth of music and literature.

Segregation

Keeping people of one skin color separate from the people of another skin color, such as having an all-black school and an all-white school.

INDEX

DATE DUE